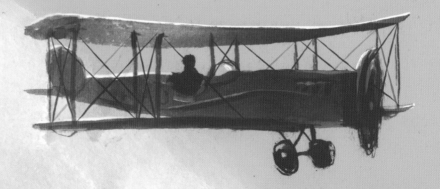

BY JILL ESBAUM

ILLUSTRATED BY STACY INNERST

JACK KNIGHT'S ★ BRAVE FLIGHT ★

HOW ONE GUTSY PILOT SAVED THE U.S. AIR MAIL SERVICE

CALKINS CREEK

AN IMPRINT OF ASTRA BOOKS FOR YOUNG READERS

New York

North Platte, Nebraska.
February 22, 1921. 10:44 p.m.

JACK KNIGHT adjusts his goggles,
eases the control stick forward, and rumbles down the runway.
Hundreds of people crowd the airstrip,
waiting in the wintry chill for . . . there! Liftoff!
Cheers ring out, and all eyes watch the plywood-covered
de Havilland until it disappears into the night.

Is Jack transporting a famous passenger?
Is he ferrying medicine to save a sick child?
Is his plane filled with precious jewels or priceless artifacts?

MARY PICKFORD

FRAGILE

Nope. So what's strapped into the open cockpit ahead of him? Six sacks of mail.

Why, then, is the crowd so excited? Because this is no ordinary mail flight. This is an all-day, all-night, coast-to-coast race to save America's struggling Air Mail Service.

Or not.

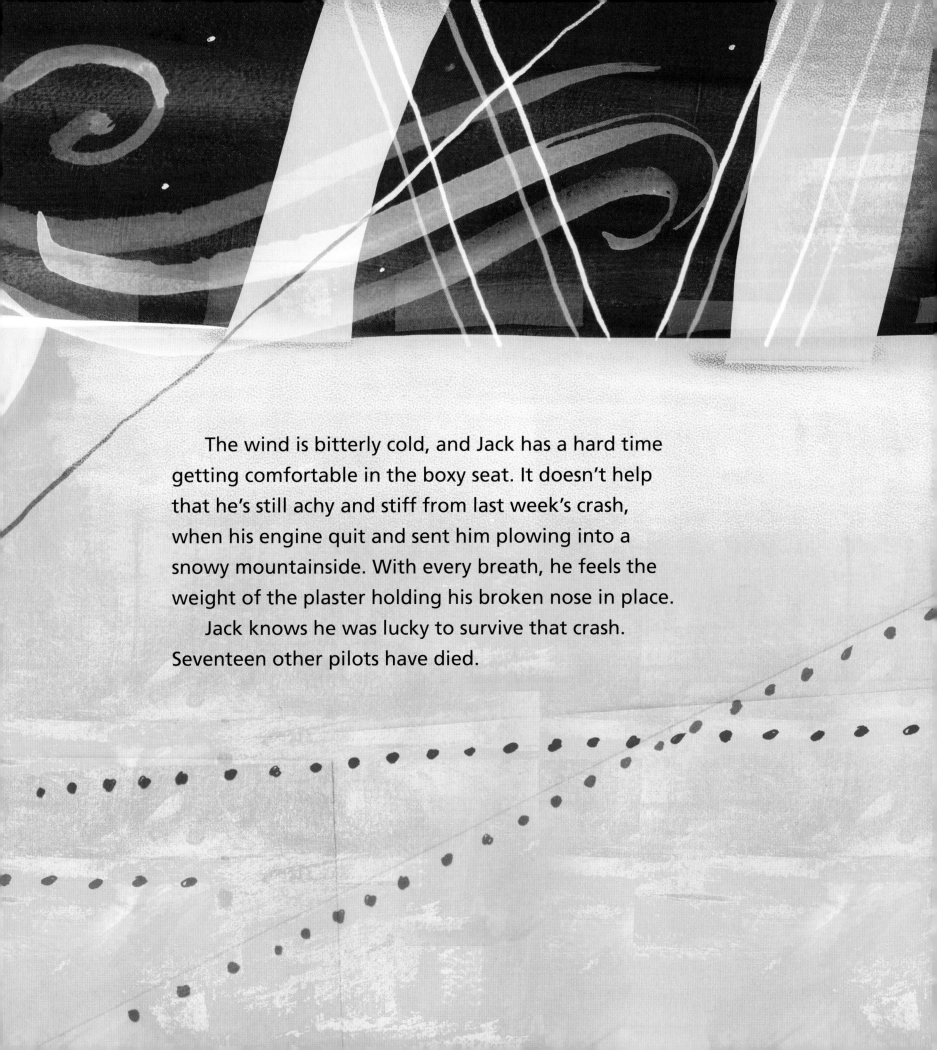

The wind is bitterly cold, and Jack has a hard time getting comfortable in the boxy seat. It doesn't help that he's still achy and stiff from last week's crash, when his engine quit and sent him plowing into a snowy mountainside. With every breath, he feels the weight of the plaster holding his broken nose in place.

Jack knows he was lucky to survive that crash. Seventeen other pilots have died.

COAST TO COAST!

CHEYENNE

SAN FRANCISCO

NORTH PLATTE

AIR MAIL RELAY ACROSS AMERICA!

Those crashes are why America's lawmakers want to end air mail. Flying is too dangerous, they say, and replacing planes costs too much. Moving mail by train is safer and cheaper.

BRAVE PILOTS RACE TO DELIVER

OMAHA

NEW YORK

★ CHICAGO

HISTORIC AIR MAIL ATTEMPT

But air mail officials—and pilots—*know* planes can move mail faster than trains. Today and tonight will prove it. Pilots are taking turns short-hopping four planes across the country, two flying east, two flying west. At least one must get through, or air mail is doomed.

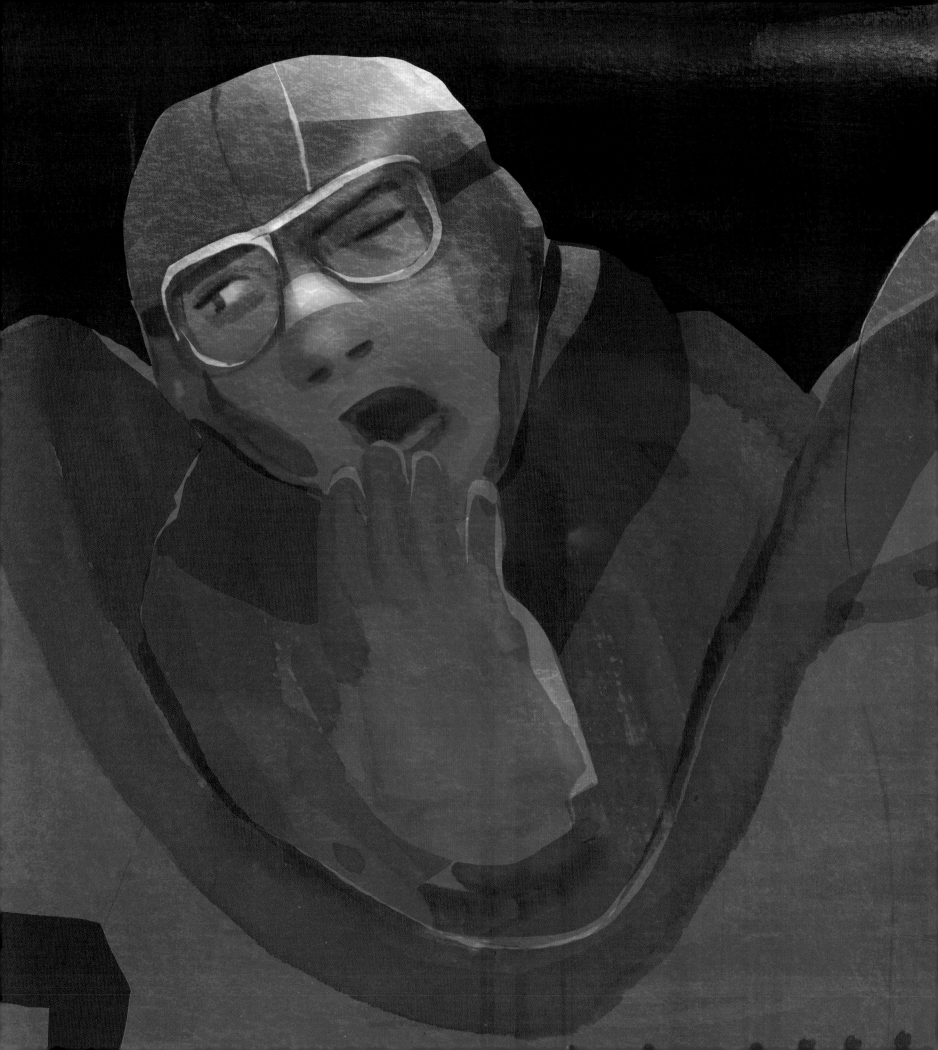

Flying the mail from Omaha to North Platte to Cheyenne, Wyoming, is Jack's regular job.

He flew the route earlier today, not knowing he'd been chosen to take part in this night flight. Now he's pooped. Oh, well. He only has to fly the 248 miles back to Omaha. As the plane drones through the night, Jack yawns and searches for landmarks below.

But nothing looks the same in the dark.

Signal fires are supposed to guide him. But it's awfully late. What if fire tenders have given up and gone to bed . . . ?

No, there's one!

Burning oil drums and torches lead Jack across
Nebraska's black prairie; past Lexington, Kearney,
and Grand Island. At last he spots a cluster of
lights. Omaha! As proud as he is to have
taken part in this relay, he's looking forward
to turning the plane over to the next pilot.

Two thousand people cheer as Jack touches down at 1:10 a.m. He drops from the cockpit, bone-tired and shivering, and is greeted with bad news: The other eastbound plane crashed in Nevada. Its pilot is dead. Another plane took its place in the relay, but now its pilot is too exhausted to continue. Worse, a blizzard has stranded the two westbound planes in Chicago.

Oh, and the pilot traveling to Omaha to replace Jack?
He can't get there, either. In this historic race across America,
Jack Knight is the relay's only hope.

You gave it your best shot, people say. Call it a night. Get some sleep.

Instead, Jack studies a road map. He wants to get a feel for the route, since he's never flown over Iowa and Illinois before. Chicago is more than 450 miles away, and at some point, he's going to collide with that blizzard.

Recalling how cold the trip has been already, he gulps hot coffee—and stuffs newspapers inside his leather suit for extra protection.

"Leave the lights on for an hour," he tells the airfield manager. "If I get lost I'll sure as heck come back."

At 2:00 a.m. Jack takes off, staying low enough to follow the barely visible tracks of the Rock Island Line. Constantly, he peers ahead for signal fires.

Jack has been in the air about an hour when he sees lights twinkling on the horizon. Is that Des Moines? Yes, there's the capitol dome! Soon, he spots the airfield. Good thing, because he's almost out of fuel.

He begins to circle . . . and his heart sinks. There's snow on the runway, and without knowing its depth, he'd be crazy to land.

All Jack can do is switch to his auxiliary tank and continue eastward. Iowa City should be less than an hour away. He'll have to refuel there.

The ground crew waiting to help Jack at the Iowa City airfield receives a telephone call from someone in Omaha telling them the relay has failed. They go home to bed.

It begins to snow. The wind shifts, slowing the plane to eighty-five miles per hour. It's a rough ride. Every jolt of the bucking plane is like a punch to Jack's aching nose.

He checks his compass often as the little plane bounces through the blizzard. Despite the cold, the engine's rhythmic throb makes Jack drowsy. His thinking . . . grows . . . fuzzy . . . *No!*

He grips the control stick with his knees and slaps his face. He leans into the icy wind and lets it scour his cheeks until the danger of falling asleep has passed.

Only a night watchman remains at the Iowa City airfield to answer a second call, reporting that the earlier message was a mistake. Jack Knight is on his way!

Jack wipes slush from his goggles. He peers ahead, but can no longer see the horizon through the swirling snow. His compass tells him he's still flying east, but . . . where's Iowa City? Will he find it before the plane runs out of fuel and crashes?

The temperature drops to −12°F. The shivering watchman stands outside a shack near the runway, listening for Jack's motor. He runs inside to warm up. Out. In. Out. Finally . . . a faint buzz. The plane! By the time he rushes to place two flares in the center of the runway, Jack is zooming in.

While the plane is being refueled, its engine running, Jack eats a ham sandwich and tries to warm up. Too soon, he's crawling back into the cockpit and taking off.

He runs into fog over the Mississippi River and climbs to five thousand feet before finding clear air. Clear, *frigid* air. Stinging his face. Stiffening his fingers. Numbing his toes.

As dawn brightens the sky, the weary pilot sees the gray smoke of Chicago factories. "It was the finest sight," he later said, "I have ever beheld."

When the plane landed at Checkerboard Field,
people rushed to congratulate Jack Knight.
Too bad he couldn't stand to greet them. His
flight suit had frozen to the seat.

3

Jack was cut from his flight suit, and his mail sacks
were transferred to another plane. One pilot flew them
to Cleveland, Ohio, and from there, another finished
the run into Long Island.

Total time for the 2,629-mile transcontinental air relay?
Thirty-three hours and twenty minutes. They'd beaten the
old plane-train record by nearly thirty-nine hours!

Jack Knight's daring, 830-mile, overnight flight made headlines across America.

Suddenly, *everybody* was excited about air mail service. Within a few days, Congress voted two-to-one to give the Service the money they needed to continue operating.

The U.S. Air Mail Service was saved, thanks to fourteen determined men who risked their lives to make it happen.

Especially one cold and exhausted hero who refused to give up.

NUTTER

HOPSON

H. SMITH

YAGER

MURRAY

WEBSTER

BLANCHEFIELD

AUTHOR'S NOTE

The mail must go through . . . but Americans couldn't always take that for granted.

Even before America's Thirteen Colonies declared their independence from Great Britain, people just as gutsy and committed as Jack Knight were striving to improve mail services. The rapid delivery we enjoy today would likely astound early colonists.

These colonists lived in isolated settlements along the Atlantic coast. When someone wanted to communicate with family—or government officials—back in England (or any other country), their letters went via ship. It took months for their letters to reach their destinations and months to hear anything back. And of course, that all depended on the ships staying afloat.

Getting mail from one colonial settlement to another was a bit speedier, thanks to trading ships that sailed up and down the coast. As new settlements popped up inland, river travelers often agreed to carry mail from town to town.

Transporting mail overland was trickier. The first dirt roads between settlements were narrow paths cut through dense forests or widened trails long-used by Native Americans. Usually, letters were sent with any traveler headed in the right direction. Successful delivery was far from guaranteed.

But early Americans knew a reliable mail delivery system was crucial to the new country's growth, and they kept working to make it affordable, faster, and more dependable.

Full-length view of U.S. Air Mail pilots James H. "Jack" Knight (left, front view) and Clarence Lange (right, back view) posed standing against a board wall at Omaha, Nebraska, to model winter flying clothing issued by the government. January 16, 1922.

Ernest M. Allison in the cockpit of his de Havilland airplane. Allison flew the final leg of the transcontinental race.

Highlights in the History of the U.S. Mail

1639 The General Court of Massachusetts names a Boston tavern as the official repository of mail to and from England and other European countries.

1673 Monthly mail transport begins between New York and Boston, via horseback. Slowly, other routes begin. Mail is dropped off in community gathering places like stores, inns, or taverns.

1753 Benjamin Franklin is one of two men appointed by the British as postmasters general of the American colonies. He establishes regular postal routes up and down the colonies. He also creates a chart that sets postal rates. Charges depend on an item's weight, listed in pennyweights, and the distance it is carried. Those charges are paid in grains of silver—often by the person receiving the letter.

1773 Once or twice a week, stagecoach drivers carry mail from town to town. They are able to carry more mail than a single rider.

1774 Unhappy with Benjamin Franklin's outspoken support of American independence from England, the British remove him from his position.

1775 The Second Continental Congress forms the Post Office Department to be headquartered in Philadelphia and names Benjamin Franklin postmaster general. Most mail is wartime correspondence between Congress and its armies as America fights to free itself from British rule.

1792 President George Washington signs the Postal Service Act, creating the U.S. Post Office Department. Part of the act states that newspapers will be carried at cheap rates so information can spread quickly. Meanwhile, sending a letter 30 miles or less costs six cents. Rates increase to a maximum of twenty-five cents for anything over 450 miles.

1811 Mail is first carried up and down America's rivers on steamboats.

1830s Trains begin transporting mail.

1840s Mail from America's East Coast arrives in California in three to four weeks when shipped to Central America, transported approximately 50 miles across Panama by mule or canoe, then put on another ship bound for San Francisco.

1852 Sending a letter less than 3,000 miles now costs three cents, if paid for in advance. If not, the charge is five cents upon delivery.

1857 Postmaster General Aaron Brown establishes four overland mail routes from the eastern U.S. to California. For many years, the Post Office pays stagecoach owners in advance for any mail they transport. It is not uncommon for those drivers to meet paying customers along the route and dump mailbags on the roadside to make room for the travelers' bags. Sometimes those discarded mailbags are picked up by another stagecoach. Sometimes they are not.

1860 Without permission from the U.S. Post Office Department, the Pony Express begins. Riders carry mail as fast as they can ride from St. Joseph, Missouri, to 165 stations across Missouri, Kansas, Nebraska, Colorado, Wyoming, Utah, Nevada, and California. Each rider gallops for about 10 miles before passing his mailbags to another rider on a fresh horse. The service goes west from St. Joseph because that is the end of the line for railroad tracks and telegraph wires. The record speed from St. Joseph to Sacramento, California, is seven days and seventeen hours. That ride takes place on November 7, and the riders carry election results: Abraham Lincoln is America's new president.

1861 Late in the year, a transcontinental telegraph line is completed. Shortly after, Pony Express delivery ends.

1863 Mail is first delivered to people's homes. Americans are now required to put street addresses on their letters. Sending one costs three cents. For the first time, customers pay for mail based only on what it weighs, not how far it's going.

1864 Nationwide, sixty-five cities offer mail delivery. Mail carriers knock, ring a bell, or whistle at a customer's door. If no one answers, the carrier tries again later in the day.

1883 The cost of mailing a letter drops to two cents.

1890 Sixty-five percent of Americans live in rural areas without mail delivery. They must pick up their mail at the nearest post office, often many miles away, whenever they can get there.

1902 Rural delivery becomes a permanent service, leading to road improvements all over America.

1911 Pilot Earle Ovington begins daily mail flights between Garden City Estates and Mineola, New York. He drops mailbags from the sky, and the Mineola postmaster picks them up off the ground. Pilots soon begin mail drops in other areas.

1918 The U.S. starts its first official air mail route between New York and Washington, D.C., using army pilots and six army training planes.

1919 A transcontinental air route is established. Short daytime hops move the mail from city to city. Mailbags are loaded onto trains for nighttime transport, since pilots can't see where they're going after dark. Sending a letter via air mail costs twenty-four cents, much higher than the ground mail rate of two cents.

1920 The Postal Service states that they will no longer allow children to be sent through the mail (by train) to visit relatives or for any other reason, even if it is cheaper than buying a ticket to ride the train as a passenger.

1921 The U.S. Air Mail Service's nonstop, coast-to-coast stunt makes history, moving mail across America in less than a day and a half. Jack Knight becomes a celebrity. More importantly, landing fields are quickly built, as are towers with lights to guide pilots flying after dark.

1923 All mail customers are required to provide mail slots or mailboxes so mail and packages can be left at a home, rather than handed to individuals personally.

1927 The government turns over its last air mail routes to private companies to fly the mail. The U.S. Air Mail Service ends.

Since Jack Knight's day, mail services have improved by leaps and bounds, thanks to innovations like ZIP codes and ingenious machines that have automated practically everything—except bringing the mail to our doors. At the time of this book's publication, first-class stamps cost fifty-five cents, and costs will undoubtedly continue to creep upward.

But if that seems expensive to you, think of it this way: Today, you can send a letter to any address in the United States for only a little over twice what it cost to do that very same thing in the late 1700s. And back then, the U.S. only had fifteen states. What a bargain!

"I got tangled up in the fog and snow a little bit. Once or twice I had to go down and mow some trees to find out where I was, but it did not amount to much, except for all that stretch between Des Moines and Iowa City. Say, if you ever want to worry your head, just try to find Iowa City on a dark night with a good snow and fog hanging around. Finding Chicago,—why, that was a cinch. I could see it a hundred miles away by the smoke. But Iowa City—well, that was tough."

"Knight's Story of Trip: Pilot Tells of Flight in Dark Through Snow and Fog."
—*The New York Times.* Feb 24, 1921, 2

BIBLIOGRAPHY

All quotations used in the book can be found in the following source marked with an asterisk (*).

EMAIL INTERVIEW

Wright, Nancy A. Editor, *Air Mail Pioneers News* (and daughter of Ernest Allison, pilot who took part in the 1921 relay across America). March 24, 2008.

BOOKS

Anderson, A. M. and R. E. Johnson. *Pilot Jack Knight*. Chicago: Wheeler Publishing Co., 1950.

Feltner, Doniv, and Starley Talbott Kassel. *Wyoming Airmail Pioneers*. Mt. Pleasant, SC: History Press, 2017.

*Rosenberg, Barry, and Catherine Macaulay. *Mavericks of the Sky—The First Daring Pilots of the U.S. Air Mail*. New York: William Morrow, 2006.

NEWSPAPERS

"Continent Spanned by Airplane Mail in 33 hrs. 20 min." *New York Times*. Feb 24, 1921: 1.

"Knight's Story of Trip: Pilot Tells of Flight in Dark Through Snow and Fog." *The New York Times*. Feb 24, 1921: 2.

Krum, Morrow. "Aviation" *Chicago Daily Tribune*. Feb 27. 1921: G5.

"Three Flyers in Cross-Country Race Here Today." *Chicago Daily Tribune*. Feb 23, 1921: 7.

INTERNET

"Airmail Creates An Industry: Knight's Night" (2004) Smithsonian National Postal Museum. postalmuseum. si.edu/exhibition/fad-to-fundamental-airmail-in-america-airmail-creates-an-industry-coast-to-coast/knights.

Fisher, Scott M. "Airmail Pilot Jack Knight's Heroic Flight in a Day-and-Night 'Grand Relay' Brought Him Instant Celebrity in 1921." archive.li/E5045.

Glines, C. V. (2006) "The Airmail Takes Wing" aerofiles.com/airmail.html.

Historian, U.S. Postal Service. "Overland Mail to California in the 1850s." August 2010. about.usps.com/who-we-are/postal-history/over-land-mail.htm.

"Jack Knight" Smithsonian National Postal Museum. postalmuseum.si.edu/exhibition/airmail-in-ameri-ca-some-early-pilots/jack-knight.

Websites active at time of publication

Keogh, Edward A. (1927) "A Brief History of the Air Mail Service of the U.S. Post Office Department." Air Mail Pioneers. airmailpioneers.org/content/Sagahistory.htm.

Lewis, Danny. "A Brief History of Children Sent Through the Mail." SmithsonianMag.com, June 14, 2016. smithsonianmag.com/smart-news/brief-history-children-sent-through-mail-180959372/.

Little, Becky. "When People Used the Postal Service to Mail Their Children." history.com, April 9, 2019. history.com/news/mailing-children-post-office.

Mola, Roger. "Transcontinental Flight and Jack Knight" U.S. Centennial of Flight Commission. centennialofflight.net/essay/Government_Role/Knight/POL4.htm.

"Pilot Stories: Knight, James H. 'Jack'" Smithsonian National Postal Museum. 2004. postalmuseum.si.edu/knight-james-h-jack.

"Rates for Domestic Letters, 1792–1863." about.usps.com/who-we-are/postal-history/domestic-letter-rates-1792-1863.pdf.

"Rates for Domestic Letters Since 1863." about.usps.com/who-we-are/postal-history/domestic-letter-rates-since-1863.pdf.

Roedel, A. E., "The Mail Must Go." *Annals of Wyoming*, Vol. 17, No. 1, 1945, pp. 64–75. archive.org/details/annalsofwyom17121945wyom.

The United States Postal Service—An American History, 1775–2006. about.usps.com/publications/pub100.pdf.

Wright, Nancy Allison. (1998) "On Wings of Faith: Navigating the First Day/Night Transcontinental" Air Mail Pioneers. airmailpioneers.org/content/milestone2.html.

———. (1998) "Remember the Air Mail Pioneers" Air Mail Pioneers. airmailpioneers.org/content/article1.html.

ILLUSTRATOR'S NOTE

My first thought when I read the story of Jack Knight was, how is it possible that this event took place 100 years ago? It was hard to believe that air mail delivery could shift from a terrifying, heroic feat to something so mundane in such a relatively short span.

As I started to research Jack's flight, I wondered how I was going to depict the sense of danger, the freezing cold, and the abject discomfort he endured in flying a wooden de Havilland DH-4B to deliver six sacks of mail at night, and in a blizzard.

My research began with watching online flight simulators and then films of pilots flying open biplanes to get a sense of how the world might have looked, sounded, and felt from Jack Knight's vantage point. I wanted to accurately depict the primitive instruments, the cramped cockpit, and the bitter cold of that open-air experience.

Nearly the entire story takes place at night, so the pictures also needed to convey the dark, remote stretches of American landscape that Jack risked his life to fly over while people slept peacefully below.

A brave flight, indeed!

ACKNOWLEDGMENTS

Many thanks to F. Robert van der Linden, PhD; Curator of Air Transportation Aeronautics Department; Smithsonian Institution, National Air and Space Museum, for his expert comments.

PICTURE CREDITS

Aviation History Collection / Alamy Stock Photo: 35. Smithsonian National Air and Space Museum (NASM 83-8165): 34.

For Will —*JE*
For Stu, Olivia, and Jake, and for highfliers everywhere —*SI*

Text copyright © 2022 by Jill Esbaum
Illustrations copyright © 2022 by Stacy Innerst
All rights reserved. Copying or digitizing this book for storage, display,
or distribution in any other medium is strictly prohibited.

For information about permission to reproduce selections from this book,
please contact permissions@astrapublishinghouse.com.

Calkins Creek
An imprint of Astra Books for Young Readers, a division of Astra Publishing House
calkinscreekbooks.com
Printed in China

ISBN: 978-1-68437-981-1 (hc)
ISBN: 978-1-63592-567-8 (eBook)
Library of Congress Control Number: 2021906401

First edition
10 9 8 7 6 5 4 3 2 1

Design by Barbara Grzeslo
The text is set in Frutiger.
The illustrations are done in watercolor, ink, pencil, rubber stamps, and some digital (Photoshop).